Keeping Me Safe At Home

The Protect Me Book Series

Written by Cindy Chambers

Illustrated By Jim Huber

First published by Dog Ear Publishing
8888 Keystone Crossing
Suite 1300
Indianapolis, IN 46240
www.dogearpublishing.net

ISBN: 978-145756-855-8

This book is printed on acid-free paper.
Printed in the United States of America

Dedication

This book is dedicated to the most precious people in our communities: the children. They should be encouraged and respectfully protected as they grow to realize as many of their dreams as possible.

This book is also dedicated to the wonderful people who devote their lives to protecting children and ensuring that they have every opportunity to grow up in a happy, safe and encouraging world.

Our Special Thanks

Our special thanks to Allyson Halverson and to Samuel Wilson for their concern for the safety of children. There positive and encouraging vision for a bright future for all children made the creation of this book possible.

Important Notes

This book is a starting point. It provides guidelines and a story to help parents and guardians better understand where to begin in putting a plan in place to help keep children safe if they need to be left home alone. This book does not pre-suppose that children should ever be left home alone. Laws and guidelines on this subject may differ in your area, so please contact your Department of Social Services for more information.

As noted above, the information contained in this book, including the story, guidelines (including child supervision guidelines), questionnaires, advice, and other content was written in collaboration with Manassas Park Department of Social Services and SCAN of Northern Virginia. It is provided as a resource to parents and/or guardians. Nevertheless, the needs of individual children or unique scenarios may require modifying the suggested guidance in the book. Parents and/or guardians should recognize that this information may not be applicable in all circumstances. The author, illustrator, publisher, and collaborators do not assume and hereby disclaim any liability to any party for any loss or damage arising from negligence, accident or any other cause in connection with the information contained in this book. Parents are responsible for the safety of their children, even if they decide to leave them at home alone.

The contents of the "Questionnaire for Family Rules" and the "Child Supervision Guidelines" at the end of the story were provided by, and will remain the property of, the organizations that provided them for the creation of this book.

Hi, I'm Oliver. I live in a neighborhood where my family has lots of friends. Our best friends are the Hernandez family. Mr. and Mrs. Hernandez have two kids, my best friend José, who is 12 years old, and his sister Ella. Ella is 9 years old, but she acts like a grown up.

One day my mom and I were asked by the Hernandez family to stop by, because they wanted to introduce us to someone who had been helping them.

As we entered the house, Mrs. Hernandez said, "This is Mr. Samuel from Child Protective Services (CPS). Mr. Samuel has been telling us how we can help keep José and Ella safe when they have to be home alone."

José jumped in and said, "Mr. Samuel taught us about how Ella and I can be in charge of stuff when we are home alone.

"We do it by making something called 'Family Rules'. I know 'rules' sound like no fun, but Mr. Samuel showed us that they're actually cool because Ella and I will be in charge of making them happen.

"Mr. Samuel said Family Rules help kids stay safe when we have to be home alone."

Right away I asked, "How did you make your Family Rules?"

José began, "First we made a list of names and phone numbers of adults that our family trusts. These are people nearby who we can call if we need help when we are alone.

"Then we decided what Ella and I would be allowed to do when we are home alone. We made rules for playing outside, doing homework, using the phone, playing with electronics, and using stuff in the kitchen.

"Mr. Samuel taught us that if someone calls when we are home alone, we should never say that our parents are not there. We should only tell the caller that our parents are busy and can't come to the phone. Then we should politely say good-bye and hang up."

"We made rules for other stuff too, like who is allowed to use the microwave and the stove.

"We decided for our Family Rules, that I can use the microwave, but Ella isn't ready for that yet. She agreed."

Right away Ella said, "Yeah, and we decided neither one of us is ready to use the stove or the oven, which is okay with us."

Ella continued, "Mr. Samuel taught us other important things to do and not to do when we are home alone. You know, like we shouldn't answer the door when we're home alone."

I asked, "José, what if I come to the door to hang out with you and I don't know that your parents aren't home?"

José proudly answered, "I will follow the Family Rules. So I won't answer the door. Then, when my parents get home, I will call you and we can hang out."

The more I was learning, the more I could see why it was important to have a parent home when friends come over.

I shook José's hand to show I was proud of him for knowing what to do.

José added, "Mr. Samuel taught us that Ella and I need to know our parents' first and last names and their cell phone numbers. We also need to know contact information for the adults that they trust."

Ella happily added, "I, of course, knew all of that information and was able to say it to Mr. Samuel the minute he asked us."

Mr. Samuel chuckled and said, "Yes, she knew the answers to all those questions, and many more."

Ella turned to me and proudly said, "When we made the Family Rules, I got a lot of responsibility too. Mr. Samuel said that's because being good at stuff sometimes has nothing to do with how old you are."

My mom and I were a little confused and asked, "What do you mean, Ella?"

Ella stood very tall and said, "Here's an example. Since I'm good at getting things done on time, that's one of the things I'm in charge of when José and I have to be home alone. Sometimes I even set a timer to make sure stuff gets done on time."

José laughed and said, "Sometimes when I'm having fun, I lose track of time. So we decided Ella gets to keep track of what time we need to do stuff, even though she's younger than me."

This stuff was starting to make a lot of sense, so I asked, "José, what else did Mr. Samuel teach you?"

José looked over the top of his glasses and said, "We learned that we need to keep doors and windows locked so we can stay safe when we have to be home alone."

That's when Mrs. Hernandez turned to my mom and said, "Mr. Samuel also taught us to let a trusted adult neighbor know when José and Ella might be home alone."

Mrs. Hernandez put her hand on my mom's shoulder and asked, "Would you be okay with being our trusted neighbor? I would like to let you know when José and Ella will be home alone. That way if you notice something that doesn't seem right, you can call me."

My mom smiled at Mrs. Hernandez and replied, "I would be happy to be your trusted neighbor."

Mrs. Hernandez explained, "We decided as part of the Family Rules, José will call me as soon as he and Ella get home from school on the days they are home alone. That way, I will know they are safe."

Then Mrs. Hernandez handed my mom a spare key to their house and said, "As our trusted neighbor, I want you to have this key in case José or Ella are ever accidentally locked out."

Of course, my mom said she would take very good care of the key and only use it in case of emergency for José and Ella.

Ella went on, "We had fun answering Mr. Samuel's questions to see what responsibilities we were ready to have for our Family Rules."

My mom asked, "What questions did you ask?"

Mr. Samuel handed my mom a paper titled "Family Rules Questionnaire" and said, "These are the questions. You should go through them with your family. The answers will become **your** Family Rules.

*The questions for creation of the Family Rules are located after the end of this story.

Mr. Samuel continued, "For example, there are questions about what your child would do if they become sick, hurt, worried or scared while home alone."

Mr. Hernandez said, "We realized that José and Ella needed to learn when it is right to call 9-1-1 and when it is not an emergency. We taught them the difference right away.

"For our Family Rules, we decided that if José or Ella is worried or scared when the two of them are home alone, they should call their mom or me right away."

My mom told Mr. and Mrs. Hernandez that she always keeps her phone charged and by her side. She said, "That way, if José or Ella need help, you can call and let me know."

Mrs. Hernandez hugged my mom and said, "Thank you."

Then my mom asked Mr. Samuel, "At what age is a child ready to be left home alone, and how long is okay?"

Mr. Samuel handed my mom a colorful chart and said, "Here are the guidelines you should follow. Oliver can read them with you."

My mom told Mr. Samuel that she liked seeing the different ages on the chart, and especially liked seeing what my age might be ready to do.

Mr. Samuel explained, "A nice lady named Miss Allyson worked with us to create the chart. She works at a place called SCAN, where they create lots of great information with us to give families."

*Child Supervision Guidelines discussed on this page are located after the end of this story.

Mr. Samuel smiled and reminded my mom that when we create **our** Family Rules, she should make sure to ask me which responsibilities I feel that I am ready for.

My mom and I were looking forward to creating our Family Rules.

As Mr. Samuel was leaving, he said, "Feel free to call me if you have any questions. CPS is here to help families keep their children safe, so if you need more help, I will be here." Then he was on his way to help other families understand how to keep their kids safe.

A couple of weeks later, José and I were playing soccer with our team. Of course my mom, Mr. and Mrs. Hernandez and Ella were there to cheer us on.

When the game ended, we were all chatting with our team members, when we saw a man walking by with his dog. It was Mr. Samuel!

Mrs. Hernandez said, "Mr. Samuel, come meet our friends!"

Mr. Samuel walked up with a big smile and introduced us to his dog, Smokey. Smokey was really nice.

Then Mrs. Hernandez and my mom introduced Mr. Samuel to everyone.

When Mrs. Hernandez explained where Mr. Samuel worked, all the parents started asking him questions about how to keep their kids safe.

That's when I had an idea.

I said, "Why don't we have Mr. Samuel come to our school and speak to everyone about how to keep kids safe when they have to be home alone? We could invite the parents to come too. That way everyone will learn."

Everyone thought that was a great idea.

My mom and Mrs. Hernandez said they would work with the principal, Mr. Samuel and me to get everything in place. José and Ella said they would help too.

I could tell my mom was proud of me for coming up with such a great idea that would help our whole community.

It was fun getting everything ready for Mr. Samuel's presentation. We even got a chance to meet Miss Allyson since she came to help.

Miss Allyson was really nice. She worked with us to make sure we had all the right information to give out to the families, teachers and students.

When the day came for the presentation, Mr. Samuel and Miss Allyson arrived early. Both of them did a great job.

The students, teachers and parents asked lots of questions. Some of the kids even gave examples of responsibilities they were ready for.

At the end of the presentation, everyone clapped and thanked Mr. Samuel and Miss Allyson. Mr. Samuel and Miss Allyson made sure to tell the parents where they could get even more information.*

Then everyone went home to make their own Family Rules. They wanted to be ready in case their kids had to be home alone.

*Parents, guardians and caregivers are encouraged to contact their local department of social services for more information on how to keep children safe.

A couple of weeks later, Mr. Samuel called my mom and Mrs. Hernandez and asked if both of our families could stop by his office.

When we got there we couldn't believe what we saw.

Mr. Samuel and Miss Allyson were sitting in a huge pile of cards and letters. The families in our community had sent the cards and letters to thank them both for coming to our school to help keep kids safe.

Mr. Samuel smiled the biggest smile ever and he and Miss Allyson said, "Thank you for helping so many families in our community."

A few weeks later, Mrs. Hernandez asked Mr. Samuel and Miss Allyson to stop by since José and Ella would be home alone. She wanted to make sure they remembered not to answer the door.

Mr. Samuel and Miss Allyson called Mrs. Hernandez later that day to tell her how proud they were that José and Ella had put their Family Rules into action, and did not answer the door.

For Parents and Guardians

When is it okay for a child to be home alone?

The "Child Supervision Guidelines" chart below was recently created by agencies across Northern Virginia to show supervision guidelines for parents to consider before leaving a child alone. These are not laws, but are recommendations.

Guidelines may differ by geographic area or region. Please contact Social Services in your area for a copy of their latest approved guidelines.

8 Years and Younger	Should always be in the care of a responsible person. Children this age should not be left unsupervised in homes, cars, playgrounds, or yards.
9-10 Years Old	May be ready to be left unsupervised up to 1.5 hours during daylight/early evening.
11–12 Years Old	May be ready to be left unsupervised up to 3 hours during daylight/early evening.
13-15 Years Old	May be ready to be left unsupervised more than 3 hours but not overnight.
16 Years and Older	May be ready to be left unsupervised overnight for 1-2 days with a plan in place.

Just because your child may be at a certain age according to the approved guidelines in your area does not guarantee that your child is ready to be left alone.

You know your child best and therefore, you should decide if your child is responsible and mature enough to be left alone, even if the chart suggests so.

You are responsible for keeping your child safe, even when you are not home.

Please remember that though these are guidelines, they need to be taken seriously.

Child Protective Services uses these guidelines as one of their tools in deciding if a child is safe or not when they get calls from concerned members of the community.

Questionnaire for Family Rules

To help determine if your child is ready to be home alone

Remember, you need to comply with local Child Protective Services Guidelines or state laws:

<u>First Considerations:</u>

- Is your child at least the minimum age to stay home alone according to local CPS guidelines or state laws?
- Is your child comfortable staying home alone?
- Does your child have disabilities or developmental delays that need to be considered?
- Does your child have mental health issues that need to be considered?
- Is your child comfortable with what to do in case of an emergency?

Note: If your child is at risk of hurting themselves or others, they cannot be left home alone.

Safety Contacts

<u>Does Your Child Know:</u>

- Their own home address
- Your first and last name and phone number
- The first and last names of trusted safety contacts
- The name of the company you work for, and what city it is in

In case of Emergency

- Make sure your child has the phone number of family or a trusted friend in case of emergency
- Arrange a certain time that your child calls you each day to ensure they are safe
- When choosing an emergency contact (EC) for your child, make sure:
  - Your child knows the EC well and is comfortable calling them
  - You are comfortable your EC is someone you would want caring for your child
  - The EC lives in close proximity to your home
  - The EC has access to transportation in case of an emergency

Health/First Aid

- Make sure you have a fully stocked first aid kit in your home
- Make sure your child knows where the first aid kit is located
- Make sure your child learns how to use the items in the first aid kit
- Make sure your child knows what to do if he/she gets sick or hurt
- If your child has a medical condition, make sure he/she understands the condition and can explain it in case of an emergency. Tape information about the medical condition to the front of your refrigerator in case of emergency
- If your child has allergies that require an EpiPen®, make sure he/she has access to an EpiPen®, has practiced with you, and is comfortable using it in case of an emergency
- Make sure that specific food or other allergens that would cause your child health issues, are not available to the child when they are left home alone

Questionnaire for Family Rules (continued)

To help determine if your child is ready to be home alone

Remember, you need to comply with local Child Protective Services Guidelines or state laws:

Dangerous Substances

- Keep alcohol, tobacco, drugs, firearms, cleaning chemicals, and other dangerous items or substances locked away and out of reach of children at all times.

Household Safety

- Do you have gas units in your home?
- Do you have working carbon monoxide detectors in the home?
- Do you have working fire/smoke alarms in the home?
- Does your child know the sound of a fire/smoke alarm or detector when it goes off?
- Are the locks on the doors and windows functioning properly?
- Does your home have an alarm system?
- Does your child know how to use the alarm system?
- What household appliances is your child allowed to use?
- Does your child know what can go in the microwave, oven and on the stovetop?
- What kitchen utensils can your child safely use when home alone?
- Does your child know who to and **not** to answer the door for when home alone?
- Does your child know what to do if someone at the door says they need help or it's an emergency?
- Does your child know who to and who not to talk to on the phone when you are away?
- Does your child know what to do if someone on the phone starts asking questions or says they need help or they are having an emergency?

Emergency Plan

- Is your child aware of all entry and exit points in the home?
- Practice safety, fire drills and the information contained in this book with your child
- Make sure your child knows where to go if there is a fire of other safety issue in the home
- Make sure your child knows how to call 9-1-1 and when it is appropriate to do so

Important

Remember to work on the answers to this Questionnaire with your family. Make sure your children know what you want them to do to be as safe as possible when you are not home. Then practice often with your family to ensure that everyone is clear about how to be as safe as possible when home alone.

The information contained in this Questionnaire is a guideline. It is not intended to be all inclusive.

Contact the Department of Social Services in your area to find out more about what you can do to keep your children safe.

The Collaborators of Our Story

Allyson Halverson (Miss Allyson):

Allyson Halverson, BS, CCLS, CTP is the Public Education Manager at SCAN of Northern Virginia, a regional child abuse prevention non-profit. Prior to joining SCAN's team, Allyson worked as a Certified Child Life Specialist and Certified Trauma Practitioner at a number of Children's Hospitals in the DC metro area to minimize trauma associated with hospitalization and medical interventions. Allyson's experience working with children following cases of abuse and neglect lead her to learn about the important preventative work of SCAN and its Public Education Program, first as a guest presenter and then as a program manager. Allyson is passionate about empowering professionals, community members, and parents by teaching them to both understand and prevent child abuse and neglect.

Samuel Wilson (Mr. Samuel):

Samuel Wilson Jr., BS, QMHP is currently employed as a Senior Family Services Specialist III with Manassas Park Department of Social Services, 1 of 120 Virginia Department of Social Services agencies across the Commonwealth of Virginia. As a certified forensic interviewer Samuel is trained to interview children who may have experience abuse, neglect or other traumatic experiences. Samuel is also trained as a Qualified Mental Health Professional. Samuel previously interned with Virginia Department of Juvenile Justice during his undergrad career. Samuel has also worked in behavioral health settings as an in-home counselor, as a support coordinator and as a supervisor. Samuel currently holds a Bachelor's Degree in Criminal Justice & Sociology from Virginia State University and is working towards his Masters in Clinical Social work at Virginia Commonwealth University. Samuel is passionate about serving children and families within his community and prevention of abuse and neglect towards children.

About Connecting with Care

Created by National Award Winning Author, Cindy Chambers, Connecting with Care creates books and other educational materials on important life subjects for children and their families.

Ms. Chambers collaborates with subject matter experts and concerned community members to bring important information to children and their families in an easy to understand and enjoyable format.

Our mission is to empower through educational materials that are encouraging and uplifting. The materials are created through collaborations with organizations and people dedicated to the health, safety and the well-being of children and their families. *Keeping Me Safe At Home* is the second book in the *"Protect Me Book Series"*. To find out more, go to connectingwithcare.com.

About the organizations that collaborated on this book

Manassas Park Department of Social Services:
Manassas Park is an independent jurisdiction in Northern Virginia, approximately 30 miles southwest of Washington, DC. The city borders Prince William County and the City of Manassas. It is primarily residential in nature within close proximity to the heart of the Greater Metropolitan Washington DC area. The City of Manassas Park Department of Social Services (MPDSS) is one of 120 departments of social services in the State of Virginia. All localities are responsible for the safety and well-being of children. Each agency offers child protection and child abuse prevention services to children and their families

MPDSS is dedicated to ensuring that children are safe and citizens are educated. Establishing safety guidelines provides guidance to ensure this happens. Our mission is to provide services and support to a diverse population who are working to achieve independence and stability. MPDSS strives to enhance the quality of life by promoting empowerment and independence through community resources and partnerships. Established safety guidelines are an essential component to this process.

Strong partnerships with The Child Protection Partnership (CPP), SCAN of Northern Virginia, local law enforcement, along with interjurisdictional relationships with surrounding localities reiterate the importance of keeping children safe.

It is the goal of MPDSS to have a positive impact on organizations and the community.

SCAN: We believe child abuse and neglect can be prevented.
For three decades, SCAN of Northern Virginia has been working throughout the region to develop effective prevention programming for all children and families, no matter what their circumstances. Our vision is a community where every child has the opportunity to grow up in a safe, stable, nurturing family, with the supports they need to thrive today and to contribute to stronger communities tomorrow.

Thanks to our donors, partners, and volunteers, we are living our mission and promoting the well-being of children. This is done by improving parent-child relations, preventing child abuse and neglect, and by educating the community about the scope, nature, and consequences of child abuse and neglect. We emphasize the importance of positive, nurturing parenting; provide direct parent education; and advocate for children in the community, the legislature and the courts.

CPSIA information can be obtained
at www.ICGtesting.com
Printed in the USA
BVHW051254270319
543782BV00001B/2/P

* 9 7 8 1 4 5 7 5 6 8 5 5 8 *